THE CUT OUT & COLLAGE BOOK

500+
AMAZING THINGS TO
CUT & COLLAGE

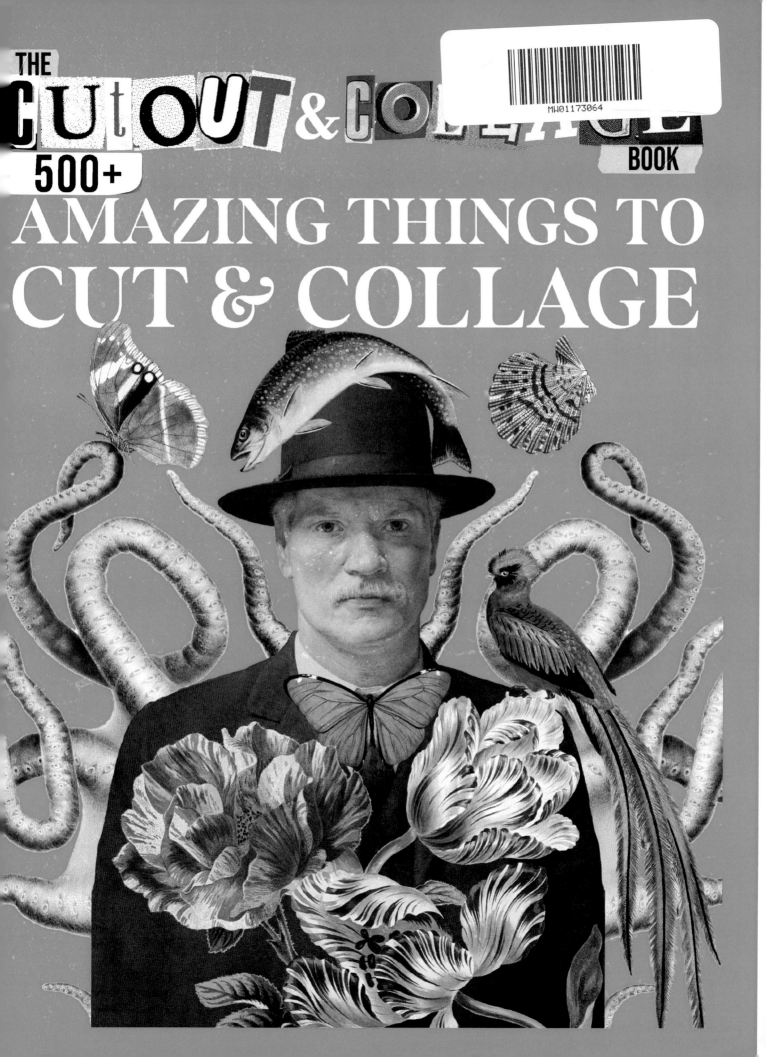

Book Content:

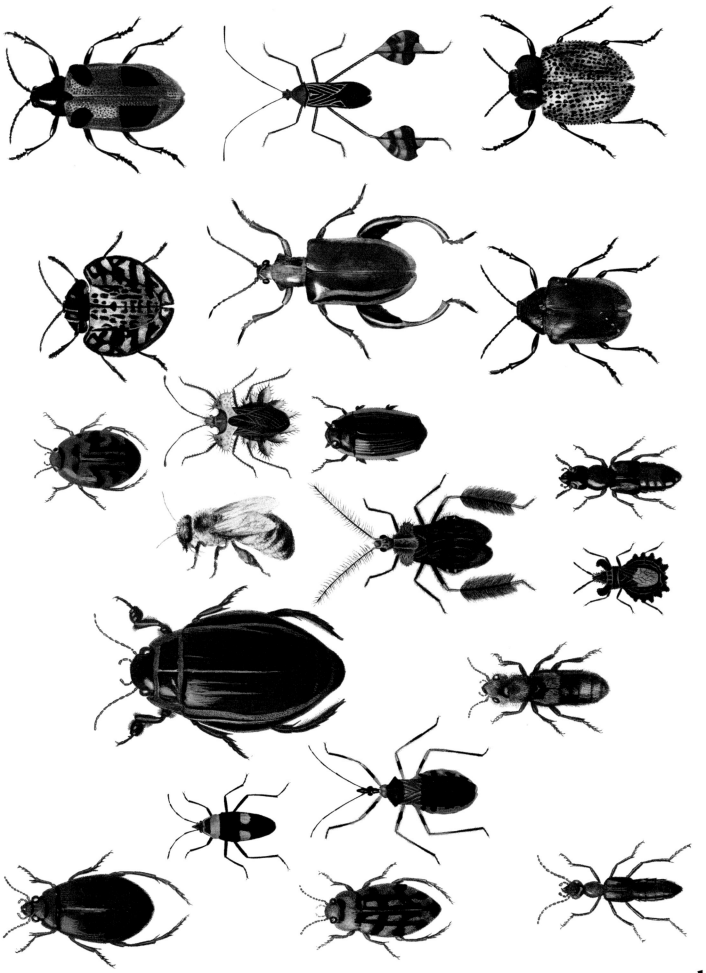

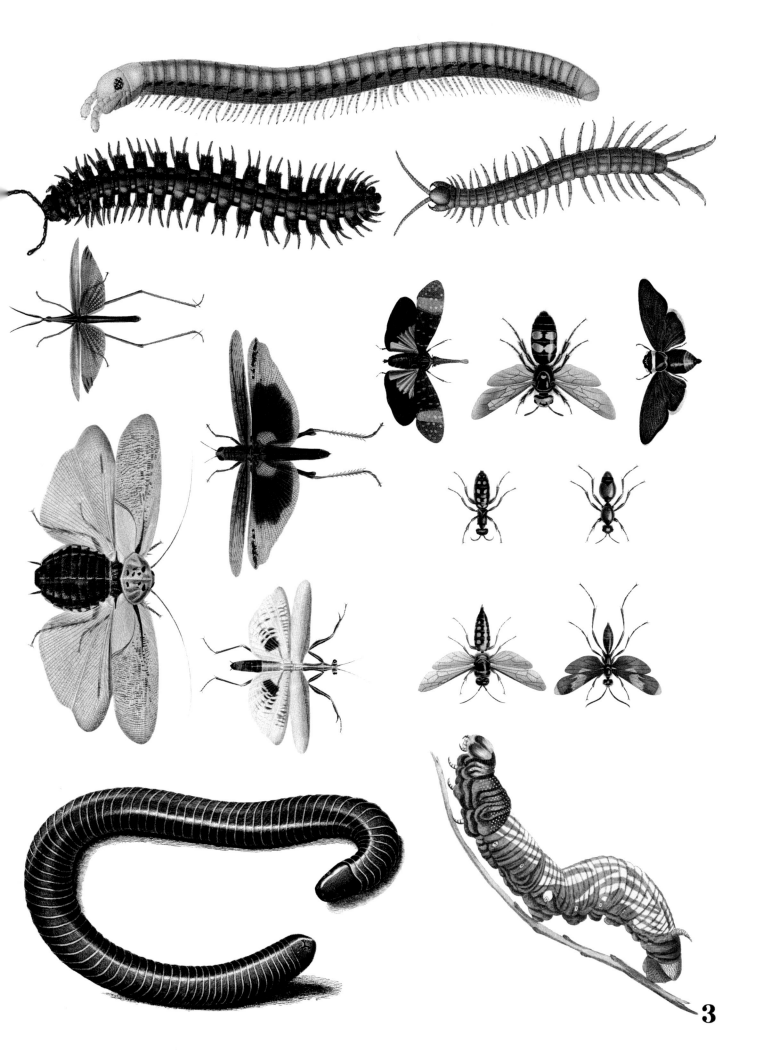

3

6

8

9

11

12

13

15

16

18

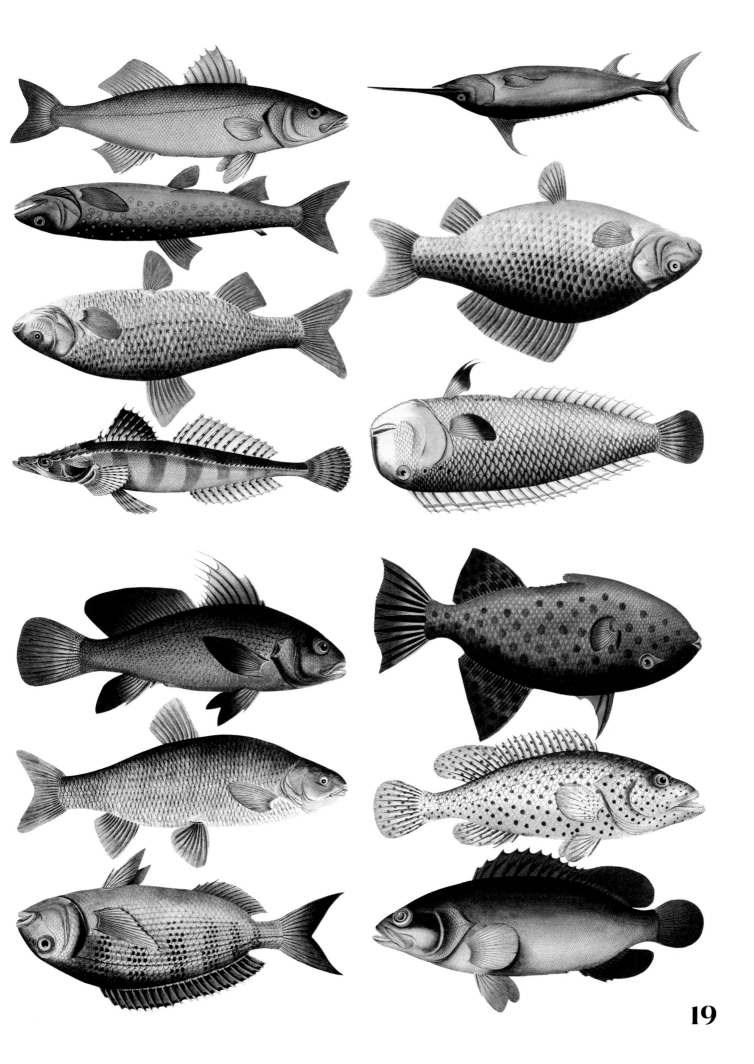

21

22

23

25

26

27

28

29

31

38

39

41

43

44

47

48

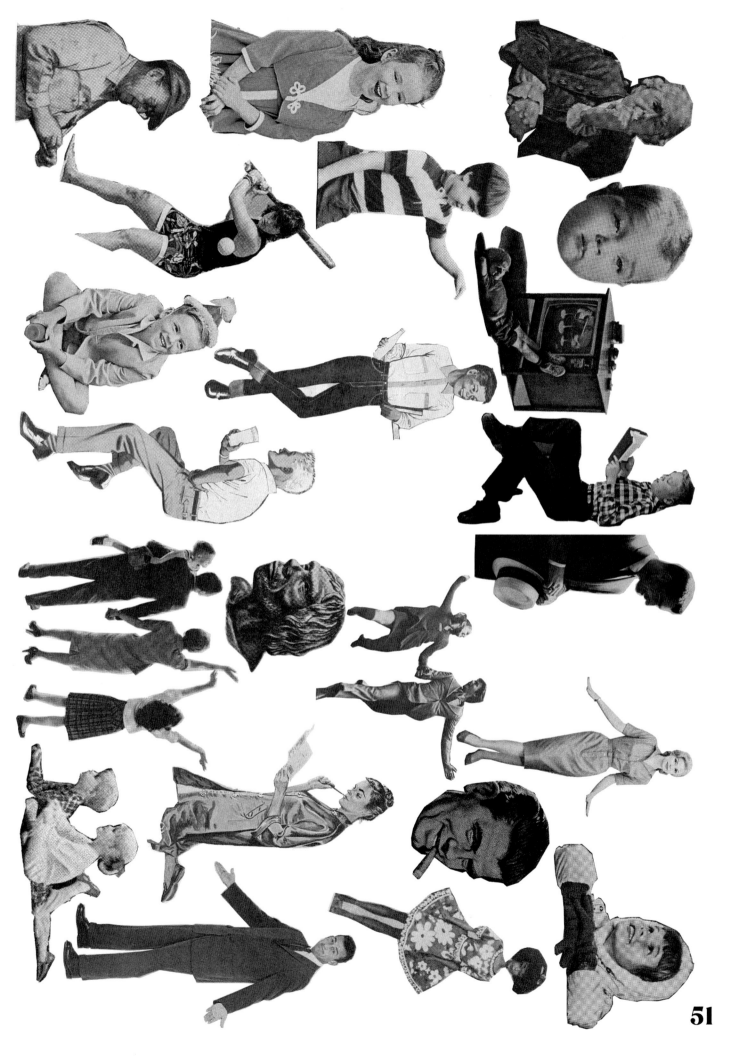

54

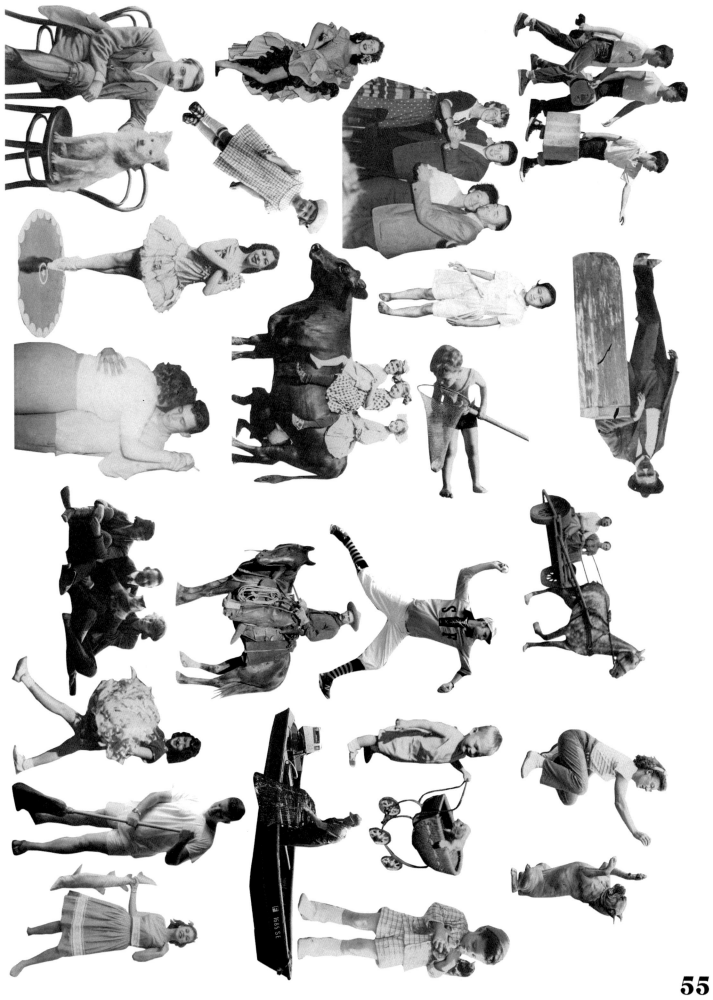

56

58

60

62

NEW ORLEANS 330 MI.

64

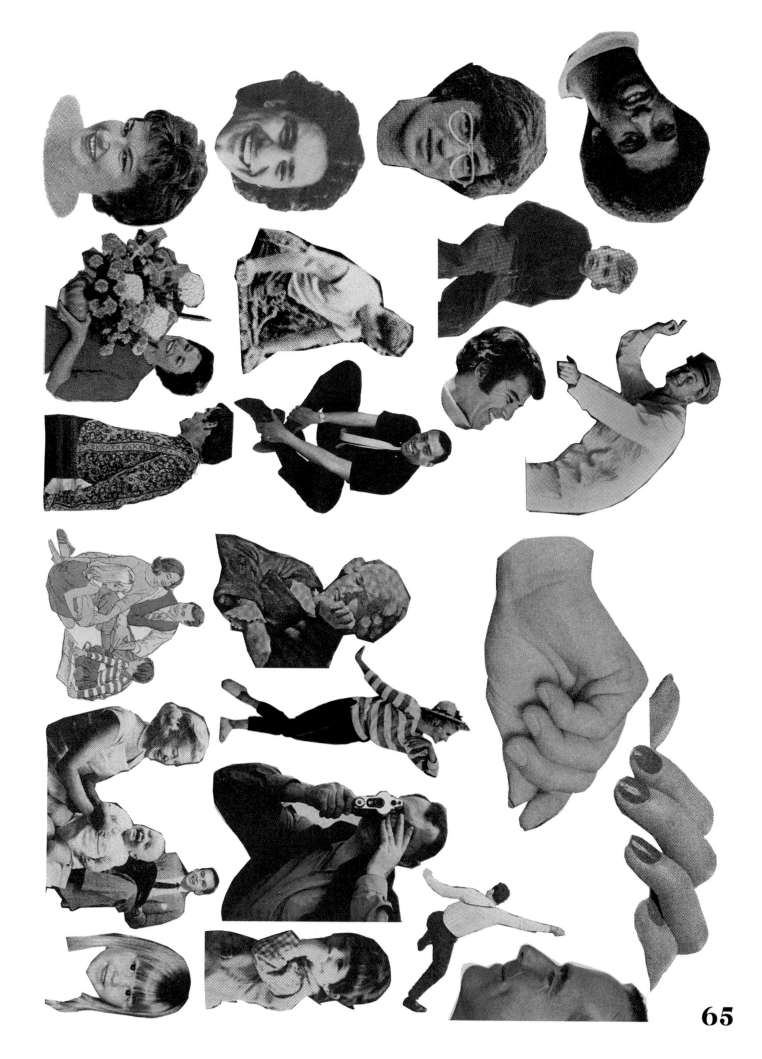

66

68

72

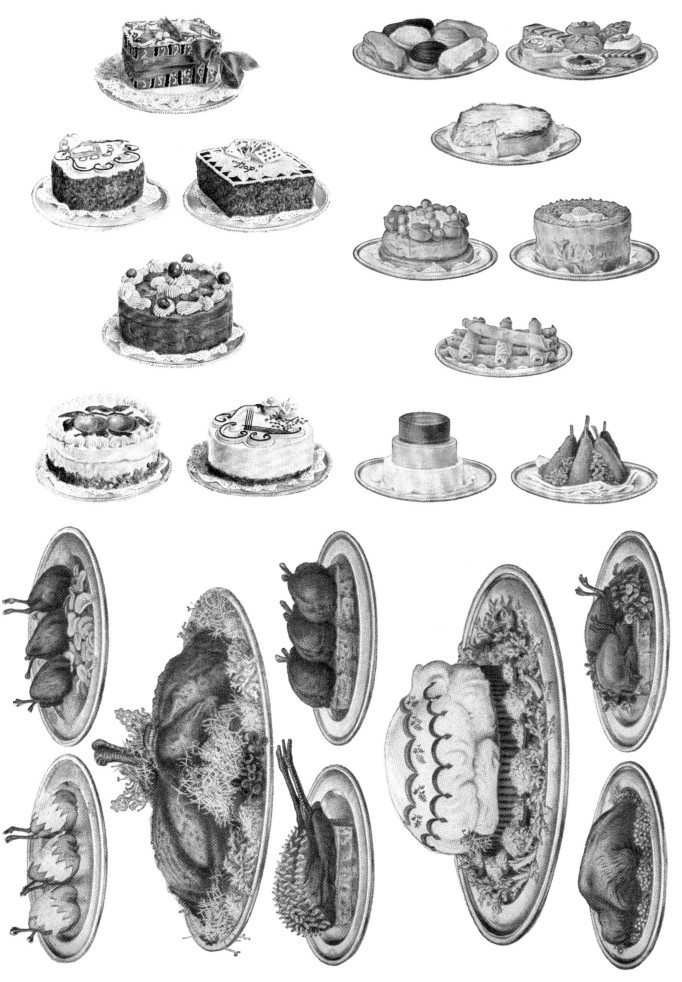

74

75

76

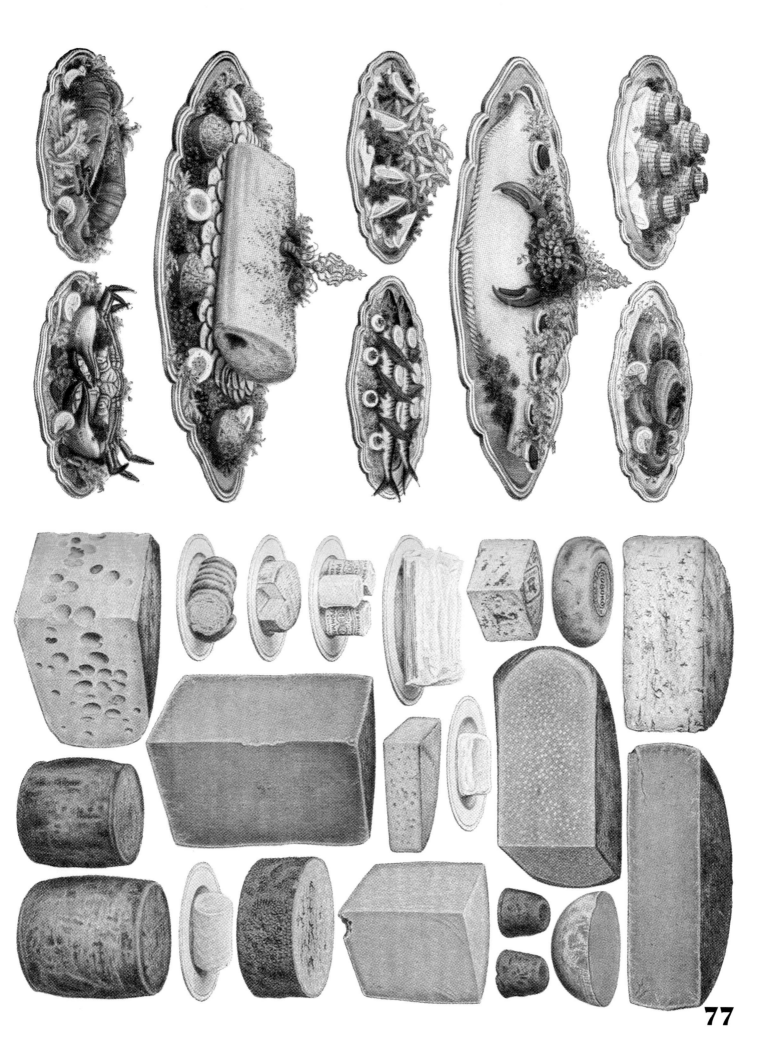

82

83

84

86

88

94

95

96

98

99

100

101

Download Your FREE Digital Collage Papers:

You Get All of the Pages inside the Book in High Quality Format!

500+ Full Color Elements From People, Animals, Flowers & Roses, Insects, Objects & More!

Scan the QR Code Below To Download The Collection:

SCAN ME

*Password: HTxVQEQqRw52FvUt

Our Other Published
Books Titles
www.collageheaven.com

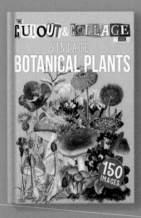

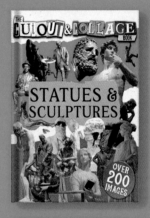

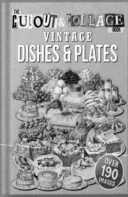

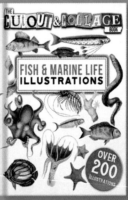
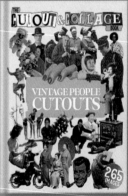

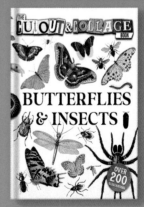

Leave us a Comment:

WE'D LOVE TO HEAR YOUR HONEST OPINION
★★★★★